LIFE ADVICE FOR THE MAN WITH A TINY PENIS

LUCAS SIMON DRAKE

WELCOME TO THE WORLD – DON'T PANIC!

If you were recently pushed out of someone's womb or dragged out into the world by the hands of a surgeon, things might be a bit chilly right now. Don't panic! Someone will soon warm your naked body up. Maybe you'll even get a nipple to suck on - I know you probably don't have teeth at the moment, but be gentle anyway! Welcome to the world. Here you'll find dogs, gossip, forests and the occasional challenge to overcome, to name a few things. There's a lot of hardship out there, but don't panic! Keep reading and we'll get the hang of this thing called life soon enough. Even if you might happen to have a tiny penis.

THE ONE TRUTH ABOVE ALL: CHANGE, THE ONLY CONSTANT

"The Only Constant in Life is Change."

- Heraclitus

There's a saying that *goes the only certainties in life are death and taxes.* For better or worse taxes look like they are here to stay, and death seems pretty unavoidable too – but the one thing that is for certain above all, no matter what, is that things will change.

Change affects the rich, the poor, famous athletes and those born left-handed, as well as the ugly, the handsome, and those who vote for the conservative political parties of the world.

Will life become better? *I don't know.*
Will life get worse? *I don't know!*
Will things change? *Certainly.*

Babies grow old, empires crumble, the stock market fluctuates, and you will be a different person tomorrow. Realise this, make this acceptance the foundation upon how you approach the world, and nothing will surprise you.

THE GOLDEN RULE:
TREAT OTHERS THE WAY YOU
WANT TO BE TREATED

Some Jewish guy with a Spanish sounding name once said *do unto others as you would have them do unto you,* and it is very good advice. If there is one rule you should take with you from this entire book, this is the one.

Disclaimer: Do you want to be whipped, gagged, and treated like a dirty little *****? Don't forget to ask for consent before treating others this way.

THE OTHER GOLDEN RULE: DON'T BE AN ASSHOLE

When I was a kid I was often a wanker. It took me until the age of 12 before I became a wanker in the literal sense, but many times I did things that made me worthy of being classed as an asshole. Today I have mostly grown out of my wanker-ism. Many people don't, and as such there are lots of assholes abound. Luckily there is a great way to decrease their numbers in the world – one way is for you to stop being one.

Whenever you are about to do something, ask yourself this one question: *By doing what I am about to do, am I needlessly being an asshole to myself or others?* If the answer to this question is yes, stop what you are doing, and pat yourself on the back for being decent. Feel free to (subtly) share this advice to the nearest asshole.

ARE YOU AN ASSHOLE?

Here's a quick little test for you to take, to see if you are an asshole or not.

- Do you drive needlessly close to cars in front of you?
- Do you have a constant need to tell people around you how incompetent they are?
- Does it seem like people are always "out to get you", just to make your day worse?
- Do you have a hard time seeing others enjoy themselves, because that makes your life seem less happy?

If you have answered yes to any of these questions, you might be an asshole. Note that there are many more asshole-things to look out for!

ON TACT

"Tact is the ability to tell someone to go to hell in such a way that they'll look forward to the trip."

- Attributed to Winston Churchill

ON BIG, LIFE CHANGING DECISIONS: MASTURBATE FIRST!

Thinking clear is important when making important choices. Having a mind clouded by horny thoughts can make for bad decisions, perhaps especially when it comes to online & offline dating. The Japanese even have a word for the clear thoughts that follows an orgasm: *Kenjataimu*.

Some cases where this might be good advice:

- When talking to people on Tinder.
- Before raiding the fridge for snacks.
- Before calling your ex.

ON WISDOM

"Knowledge is knowing that you can put a light bulb in your mouth and that taking it out will break it. Wisdom is to never put light bulbs in your mouth in the first place."

- Random Redditor

ON DRIVING IN TRAFFIC: ASSUME EVERYONE IS OUT TO KILL YOU

Set your timer for one hour and start snapping your fingers one time for every passing second. For each snap, that's one person dead per day around the globe in a traffic accident. Annually, that makes for some 1.35 million people. Quitting your snapping won't save any lives, but if you assume that every person and their mother on the road is out to kill you, you might avoid becoming a part of the worrisome statistics.

A few tips for making it to the age of autonomous cars:

- Stop signs, like all other signs, are just signs - not a guarantee that people will obey them.
- Assume that you are invisible – especially if you are on a motorcycle.

- Let idiots pass.
- Assume that the Skoda ahead will cut you off.

ON COMPARING YOURSELF TO OTHERS

"Comparison is the thief of joy."

- Attributed to Theodore Roosevelt

It is a common belief that people think other people spend more time partying, hiking, and being successful than they themselves do – and social media isn't making this belief less common.

Compare yourself to Gordon Ramsey, and you are a lousy chef. Compare yourself to Marie Curie, and your contributions to science feel lackluster. Compare yourself to that one social-butterfly on your Instagram-feed, and you're a loner. Compare yourself to Neil Armstrong, and you are a worthless astronaut.

The feelings of inadequacy we feel when comparing our lives to other's might exist because at some point in our evolution, a competitive mindset made it so that one would work harder to acquire more resources and therefore having better prospects of procreating.

We are the same people as our ancestors, only living in a much more complex society today – back then we compared ourselves to those we knew, because those were all the people we knew about! Were you good at something, you were likely the person in the tribe known for being good at just that. *"What a spear-tosser Grok is!"*

Today our social networks are larger, and athletes, movie stars and entrepreneurs are those we compare ourselves too. Stop comparing yourself to them, and instead see how you can improve upon the person you were yesterday – if improvement is your goal. If you manage to delete Instagram from your phone, that's a plus.

ON FINDING YOUR SOLE MATE

"Walking is too big a part of life to buy shoes without trying them on first."

- Anyone with feet

ON SITTING TOO MUCH

I know, I know – humans today are an inactive species. But hey, at least I run on Saturday mornings, so that's good, right? Yeah, it is. But you're still likely moving to little, if your work consists of you sitting in a chair all day.

Studies have shown that vigorous physical activity does not do away the negative health impacts of prolonged sedentary time during the day – your flexibility is still getting tanked, your health markers are slowly getting worse, and your bones weaken when they aren't getting used enough, leading to an increased risk of injury – and death – at an advanced age. Physical activity is something we need on the daily. So get out of that "ergonomic" chair twice an hour, and move them legs.

ON POOPING WRONG

What? I have to be stressed out over how I poop now? No, you don't. You are likely a perfectly adequate pooper – but not great, if you live in the west. Because we poop wrong.

Sitting on a seat with our legs at a ninety-degree angle compared to shitting in a squat-position will make it much easier to squeeze them logs out. This helps prevent constipation, which in turn will make it much less likely for you to develop hemorrhoids and anal fissures. Nobody wants those.

Start squatting, or buy yourself a squatty-potty to rest your feet upon. Guests might think it silly, but you will never want to poop anywhere else again – trust me on this: your anus will thank you.

ON KEEPING YOUR
PHONE IN THE BEDROOM

You wouldn't tell someone addicted to heroin to keep a few hits next to bed, so why are you doing basically the same thing each night? Here is why you should kick the phone out of your bedroom:

- You will sleep better when the screen's light isn't messing with your circadian rhythm.
- You might actually spend quality time with a partner – who knows, you might even get laid!
- Being offline will not kill you.
- You will sleep longer, and your days will be more enjoyable because of it.

Kick that phone out!

ON TAKING ILLICIT DRUGS.

I'm not here to judge – sometimes people enjoy things that others think are inappropriate, like certain drugs. I do not condone the use of illicit substances of any kind, but I do want you to say safe in whatever you are doing.

Here are a few tips to use drugs in a safe manner:

Druggie-tip #1:
Don't do stupid shit.

Druggie-tip #2:
***Don't do stupid shit**. There, now I've said it twice.*

I bet a bunch of you are gonna ignore this shit though, right? Don't.

Druggie-tip #3:

Have a sober friend with you.

Having someone with a clear mind will help make things keep safe. Yes, on LSD you might feel that your heavy clothes are pushing you down to the centre of the Earth, but if it's cold a sober friend might be able to help you focus on something else – so that you don't get naked in the middle of the nettle-oak ridden bush.

Besides, who is gonna be able to re-tell all the stupid and funny shit you did if everyone around you is high as a kite?

"Did you guys hear what Zeke did last night during his heroic mushroom trip? He had super-fun and came up with some stupid, but kinda-hilarious ideas on the human psyche. Jimmy told me, he was trip-sitting him!"

"That sounds like a great, responsible time! Jimmy is great at keeping you grounded. I should tip sit for him some time!"

Druggie-tip #4:

Test your stuff!

The internet is great, partly because you can order drugs of it if you know how – and it is equally awful for the same reason. Something that is really great about the internet? You can order drug testing kits from there! Note: Don't forget that dark-web reviews are important!

Are you about to drop LSD? Head straight on over to *bunkpolice.com* and buy some *Erlich's regent.* Making the night out a bit more fun with some cocaine? **Buy a fentanyl strip**. That shit is getting into more and more drugs – don't risk your life when you can test your stuff for about a dollar.

"A dollar spent on a fentanyl testing kit, is nine-thousand dollars saved on a funeral!

- Someone wise

Druggie-tip #5:

Set & setting

Some drugs, particularly the psychedelic ones, are really good at putting the mind into an altered state, which is why they are so popular. The mind becomes very malleable and open to ideas on them, which means can be good as we can see life in a new light. But it can also mean heavy burdens on our body and soul can affect us more than usual.

Set is the mindset of they who goes on any trip. Are you currently going through something hard, that you have had a hard time dealing with even while sober? You might want to be in a more stable state of mind before heading out on any psychedelic adventures.

Setting is the psychical and social environment you are in. If you are in alone in a big city, the setting might not be optimal. Together with a friend out in a wonderful nature-reserve, where you are certain you won't be disturbed by others? That sounds lovely. Remember to keep Druggie-tip #1 in mind.

ON APPLES

"An apple a day keeps the doctor away. Throw it hard enough, and it keeps anyone away."

- Anonymous Philosopher

ON HITTING CHILDREN

When you hit a child, you teach them a lesson. Not the lesson you intend to teach, but instead you teach them not to trust you, and to better hide what causes you anger.

Don't hit children – *also see "the other golden rule".*

ON USELESSNESS

"There is nothing so useless as doing efficiently that which should not be done at all."

- Peter Drucker

ON SHOWER SEX

There are some great uses of showers when it comes to getting orgasms. Pressurized shower heads? Check! Privacy? Check! Falling water that can mask sound? Check! Great for good-old-fashioned, penetrative sex? Eh...

Some movies show shower sex as a hot and steamy thig for couples to rock each other's socks off – but reality shows that the shower isn't that great for the most common type of sex where a phallic object stuck to a person penetrates another someone in some way. A slippery floor and falling water removing any natural lubricants makes this fun-to-do-in-theory thing a not-as-fun thing to do in practice, especially if the height difference is big.

So if you are disappointed by not enjoying shower sex as much as you'd like to, don't worry – you're not alone.

ON WISDOM (AGAIN)

"Knowledge is knowing tomato is a fruit. Wisdom is to not use it in a fruit salad."

– Attributed to Miles Kingston

ON BEARS

Out in bear country? Awesome! Bears live in some beautiful places, so I am happy you're getting out there. Here are some tips on how to stay safe when hanging out with Baloo & Gang:

Bear-tip #1
Be noisy!

This does not mean sharing your awful taste in music with the world with those awfully loud speakers, but rather that you should alert the bears of your presence by clapping, singing or calling the little buggers out every once in a while.

"Hey little bear, I am here!" called the hiker who lived.

"…" said the silent, grumpy hiker who became bear poop.

Bear-tip #2

Stay together!

Having a few friends with you out in the woods can be a good thing, especially if one of them is slower than you – who knows when you guys will be chased by some 400-pound, cuddly predator?

There is safety in numbers apart from having a sacrificial friend – the more you are, the more likely it is that a will hear you chat, and the less likely it is to challenge you. Bears can't do calculus, but they can count.

Bear-tip #3 *Use a bear canister*

Bears love food, and their creativity in acquiring it from unprepared humans is boundless. Luckily humans are nifty too, which is why bear canisters exist. Don't keep food in your tent, don't hang it in a nylon bag in a tree, don't hide it under your friend's pillow – use a bear canister, and your trail food will remain yours. Remember to store and eat food a good distance away from any camp.

Bear-tip #4 *Back away slowly and sideways*

If you see a bear, you should get away. It will probably run away first, but if it remains stationary looking at you, it's your move. Don't run, unless you want the bear to see you as prey.

Back away slowly and sideways so you won't trip on anything unexpected. If it hasn't seen you – stay silent until it's far away. If it is aware of your presence - speak calmly to it as you move away. ***Do not drop your pack!*** If it decides you look like someone to mess with, it can offer protection.

Bear-tip #5

When a bear attacks:

Black bear attacks are simple – if they decide to advance, stand your ground and intimidate them. Get big, get loud, and get amped up and ready to fight back. If you have bear-spray and the bear charges, now is the time to spray. It is your best defence against a charging bear, but you've got to fight it – aim for the face and muzzle with any objects you have available.

Brown & Grizzly bears: if it charges, play dead by laying on the ground with your hands clasped above your head for protection, and legs spread wide so it can't easily flip you over. Lay still until it walks away – but if the attack persists, it's time to fight back with all you've got. Make loud noises, aim for the face and muzzle, and pray that the bear gets a sudden urge for berries or salmon instead.

ON STICKING
STUFF UP YOUR BUTT

I have a few friends in the medical field, and each and every one of them has some stories to tell on this. The amount of people – mostly men – who come in with strange things up their butts is staggering. If you ever decide to put anything in your butt, have it be something with a flared base.

For the love of all that is holy, make sure anything you stick up your butt has a flared base.

ON LOSING WEIGHT

Do you want to lose weight? Great, read on! Happy with how things currently are? Even better!

To lose weight, and by weight we mean body fat, you must keep a negative energy balance. It is boring sounding, **but it applies to everyone**: it's all about calories in, and calories out. Spend more energy than you consume.

Here are a few tips on how to do this:

- **Counting calories** (and eat less food): if you are not doing this, you cannot be sure that you are taking in fewer calories than you expend.
- **Move more**: exercise, go for hikes, run, swim, walk on your hands.. making it fun and lasting be more important than looking for the exercise

that gives the most bang-for-your-buck calory-wise.

- **Exclude food groups**: go vegetarian, eat less fat, fewer carbs – it's all about getting a negative energy balance, weight-wise.

- **Sustainability is key**: certain diets will be harder to keep than others. Foregoing carbs might be great for stable insulin levels, but if your diet isn't sustainable and you keep caving in because of societal pressures or because you live next to a bakery, try something else.

ON GAINING WEIGHT

Do you want to gain weight? Great, read on! Happy with how things currently are? Even better!

To gain weight, and by weight we mean body fat (and maybe some muscle), you must keep a positive energy balance. It is boring sounding, but it applies to everyone: it's all about calories in, and calories out. Consume more energy than you spend.

Here are a few tips on how to do this:

- **Counting calories** (and eat more food): if you are not doing this, you can not be sure that you are taking in more calories than you expend.
- **Move less**: don't exercise, don't go for hikes, don't run, don't swim, don't walk on your hands..

- **Include more food groups**: don't go vegetarian, eat more fat, more carbs – it's all about getting a positive energy balance, weight-wise. Just eat everything, and more of it.

- **Carbs and sugars are your friend:** especially sugar is great for gaining weight because you can never have enough. It's hard to consume 2000 calories of steak, but gobbling down on the same number of calories on pizza or a sweet milkshake is something much more achievable. Not saying it's healthy, but it will help you put on those pounds.

ON LIVING LONGER

Here are a few things to do in order to live longer:

- **Don't be male:** women tend to live longer.
- **Lose weight**: light people's cells aren't dividing as often as heavy people's cells, and cells can only divide so many times – as of now, at least.
- **Be healthy:** getting sick and dying is not great for longevity. Don't do stupid shit: this especially applies to young men. Roof-top parkour is fun, but not great as a life-extension therapy.
- **Hope for a scientific breakthrough**: if you are young enough, we might see some interesting scientific discoveries on how we can reverse aging in the future. If you are old already, you might have missed the *live-almost-forever boat* (which may or may not ever arrive).

ON WHAT TO READ NEXT:

This is the last page of the book. Unless you want your brain to atrophy as be the size of a peanut, you should keep reading other books.

Here's an outtake of a book I wrote about running a 50-mile ultramarathon on LSD – which by the way is something you should probably not do. Here's the introduction to *Runner's High: or Can LSD Make You Gay? Enjoy.*

RUNNER'S HIGH: OR CAN LSD MAKE YOU GAY?

I could not move my gaze from his butt. The cheeks were like two bowling balls of pure muscle sculpted by Michelangelo himself. They were firm, yet at the same time bouncy.

It had taken me over two and a half decades of denial, a race twice as long as a regular marathon and two hundred micrograms of LSD to realize what was now obvious.

I was gay.

A MONDAY MORNING, 2017

"Unless you are Kenyan it's stupid to even try." Linda said. "It can't be healthy to run that far!" The discussion in the break room during lunch had veered into one about marathons after a coworker had finished one during the weekend.

"Come on, running is good for you!" Peter remarked.

"Maybe some jogging, but a marathon? That isn't natural. My cousin ran the New York Marathon, guess what happened to her? Threw up at the finish line, spaghetti-legs for days!"

"Well, there are those who think humans are amongst the best runners in the world and that running is something that comes naturally to us." I chimed in.

"Best in the world? Right! I'd like to see you run as fast as Philip!" Linda exclaimed, referring to her dog.

"I think Lucas is right here," Peter said. "I've heard this too, that there are people from an Indian tribe somewhere in Mexico that can run for hours and hours without getting tired."

"Well, if only we were all Indians!" Linda said and smiled, then left the break room. Linda liked three things more than anything else in her life: her dachshund Philip, talking about her dachshund Philip, and being right. So whenever she sensed that a conversation was leading into territory that would question her beliefs, she would either talk about Philip, or leave the room.

"It's true what you say, about people running for hours and hours," I said to Peter. "Even days! There are plenty of races around the world that are longer than marathons."

"I've heard about those. Though I think you have to be crazy to do that. Just because you can do something doesn't mean you should!"

"Probably not," I replied. "But it would be cool to say you've done such a thing! Something to cross off your bucket list if you get some terminal disease, you know?"

"I know what I would do if I had a terminal disease," Peter said.

"What's that?" I asked him.

"Take a shit-ton of drugs" he answered. "Or you know what? Maybe I'd run one of those really long races while taking a shit-ton of drugs."

"That's why they call it a runner's high!" I answered

him, and we both laughed. "All this talk kinda makes you want to get a terminal disease."

"The good thing about doing stupid things on drugs is that you can do it even if you're not terminally ill. Get busy living or get busy dying, you know?"

Back at my desk I started thinking about what Peter had said to me. Then I got a brilliant idea.

***

Runner's High: or Can LSD Make You Gay? is available as an e-book and as a paperback and hardcover book on Amazon.

Other books for people with and without penises written by Lucas Simon Drake:

- Life Advice for the Man With a Huge Penis
- Donald Trump: Life Advice From Me to You
- Queen Elizabeth II - A Monarch's Long Life in Brief

Printed in Great Britain
by Amazon

14587813R00037